This Jou

with love for:

_____

This Journal is my gift to you, my sweet grandchild. It is a keepsake of my life & memories that I hope you will treasure forever.

When & where I was born, where I grew up, where I went to school, ...

_____

_____

_____

_____

_____

_____

_____

_____

_____

_____

_____

_____

_____

What I looked like before you were born (add picture):

What I want you to know about our family heritage ….

"Nobody can do for little children what grandparents do. Grandparents sort of sprinkle stardust over the lives of little children." Alex Haley

My earliest & best childhood memories include …..

_____

_____

_____

_____

_____

_____

_____

_____

_____

_____

_____

_____

_____

"It is a smile of a baby that makes life worth living."
Debasish Mridha

This is what I liked to do as a kid .....

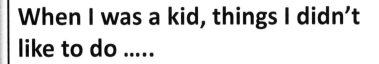

When I was a kid, things I didn't like to do …..

_____

_____

_____

_____

_____

_____

_____

_____

_____

_____

_____

_____

_____

"I know what it is like to be brought up with unconditional love. In my life that came from my grandmother." Andre Leon Talley

My first job, and other jobs I have since had, and what my jobs taught me .....

_____

_____

_____

_____

_____

_____

_____

_____

_____

_____

_____

What I want you to know about my parents (your great-grandparents) such as DOB, place of birth, personalities, etc. …..

_____

_____

_____

_____

_____

_____

_____

_____

_____

_____

_____

_____

_____

How I met your grandfather, and how our life together started (our children, their DOB, our first home, etc.) .....

_____

_____

_____

_____

_____

_____

_____

_____

_____

_____

_____

Grandchildren make life complete.

Special skills I have, hobbies I like to do, and talents I have include .....

_____

_____

_____

_____

_____

_____

_____

_____

_____

_____

_____

_____

_____

_____

My hopes and dreams for you include .....

_____

_____

_____

_____

_____

_____

_____

_____

_____

_____

_____

_____

10 random things that you might like to know about me (i.e. name of my first pet) .....

_____

_____

_____

_____

_____

_____

_____

_____

_____

_____

_____

_____

**Great things come in
small packages.**

My favorite music – songs, artists were/are .....

_____

_____

_____

_____

_____

_____

_____

_____

_____

_____

_____

Funny stories from when I was growing up .....

"Children see magic
because they look for it."
Christopher Moore

More favorite memories I have of growing up .....

_____

_____

_____

_____

_____

_____

_____

_____

_____

_____

_____

What I want you to know about what life was like when I was growing up & before you were born .....

_____

_____

_____

_____

_____

_____

_____

_____

_____

_____

_____

_____

A funny or memorable story about your mother/father is .....

_____

_____

_____

_____

_____

_____

_____

_____

_____

_____

_____

_____

"Nanas hold our tiny hands for just a little while, but our hearts forever." Unknown author

Something that I learned the hard way was .....

_____

_____

_____

_____

_____

_____

_____

_____

_____

_____

_____

_____

_____

Where I have lived throughout my life (include addresses, if available), and here is a description of my homes ....

_____

_____

_____

_____

_____

_____

_____

_____

_____

_____

_____

"Grandparents make the world a little softer, a little kinder, a little warmer."
Author unknown

My favorite toys and games as a kid included .....

_____

_____

_____

_____

_____

_____

_____

_____

_____

_____

_____

_____

_____

The best lessons that I have learned in life include .....

_____

_____

_____

_____

_____

_____

_____

_____

_____

_____

_____

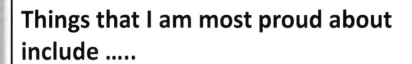

Things that I am most proud about include .....

_____

_____

_____

_____

_____

_____

_____

_____

_____

_____

_____

_____

_____

"A grandparent is a little bit parent, a little bit teacher, and a little bit best friend."
Author unknown

**My favorite vacations include(d)
.....**

_____

_____

_____

_____

_____

_____

_____

_____

_____

_____

_____

My favorite memories of your mom/dad include .....

"Grandchildren are the dots that connect the lines from generation to generation." Lois Wyse

My memory of the day you were born .....

Hardships that my parents went through or that I went through in life .....

_____

_____

_____

_____

_____

_____

_____

_____

_____

_____

_____

_____

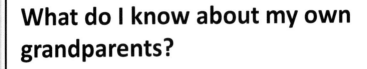

What do I know about my own grandparents?

"My grandchild has taught
me what true love means."
Gene Perret

The most important things in life are and the reasons why .....

_____

_____

_____

_____

_____

_____

_____

_____

_____

_____

_____

_____

_____

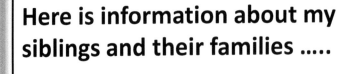

Here is information about my siblings and their families .....

Before you were born, this is what was going on in the world news, music that was popular, etc. .....

_____

_____

_____

_____

_____

_____

_____

_____

_____

_____

_____

_____

"A grandchild fills a space in your heart that you never knew was empty."
– Unknown

My favorite season, time of day, friends, things to say, etc. .....

People I find inspirational and the reasons why include .....

"If I could reach up and hold a star for everytime you've made me smile, the entire evening sky would be in the palm of my hand." Author unknown

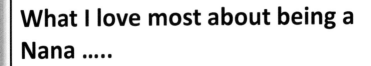

What I love most about being a Nana .....

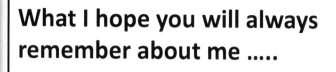

What I hope you will always remember about me .....

"A child reaches for your hand, and touches your heart." Author unknown

This is my love letter to you, my grandchild ….. (what I love about you, what I see as your special talents, etc.)

_____

_____

_____

_____

_____

_____

_____

_____

_____

_____

_____

"If I had known grandchildren were this much fun, I would have had them first." – Unknown

Child of my child, heart of my heart. Your smile bridges the years between us...
I am young again, discovering the world through your eyes. You have the time to listen and I have the time to spend, Delighted to gaze at familiar, loved features made new in you again. Through you, I see the future. Through me, you'll see the past. In the present, we'll love one another as long as these moments last.
— Author Unknown

Made in the USA
San Bernardino, CA
25 November 2019

60390395R00069